Your Business Sweet Spot

**SIMPLIFY YOUR BUSINESS.
AMPLIFY YOUR RESULTS.**

RACHEAL COOK MBA

Copyright (c) 2016 Racheal Cook MBA | The Yogipreneur LLC

All rights reserved. No parts of this book may be reproduced in any form without permission in writing from the author. Reviews may quote brief passages in reviews.

The Yogipreneur LLC
9702 Gayton Road Suite #154
Richmond, VA 23239 United States

Contents

Intro — 1

How to Use This Book — ix

PART 1:: YOUR BUSINESS SWEET SPOT

Chapter 1:: Birth of The Business Sweet Spot — 15

Chapter 2:: Your Passion — 27

Chapter 3:: Your Purpose — 35

Chapter 4:: Your Prosperity Plan — 45

Chapter 5:: Articulating Your Business Sweet Spot — 59

PART 2:: DISCOVER YOUR BUSINESS SWEET SPOT

What Is Your Business Sweet Spot Theme?	72

PART 3:: ALIGNING WITH YOUR SWEET SPOT

Maker	77
Maven	99
Mentor	117
Mastermind	137
About The Author	155
More From Racheal Cook	157
Take The Quiz	159
Deep Gratitude	161

Intro

Francesca was living the ultimate yoga teacher dream.

Over nearly ten years, she had built a lucrative private yoga business, teaching up to 25 private students per week in New York City. One day would bring her to the financial district, where she would help executives find some peace in the corporate gym. The next, she'd be in someone's beautiful home helping them to strengthen and heal their bodies.

And while she adored her clients, over time the crazy schedule and often 80+ hour weeks started to wear her down.

Francesca ran into a classic challenge that

so many entrepreneurs find themselves in – she was overworked, over-scheduled, and exhausted.

She was trapped by her own dream business.

It seems like everyone's talking about following your passion to create a business and life you love… but how exactly do you DO that?

You'd think with all the information available at our fingertips, it'd be easy to figure it all out on your own, right?

Not quite.

Just knowing where to start is overwhelming to most hopeful entrepreneurs. Do you need to first get a website – or should you just start talking to people? Should you just start working 1×1 or should you first create a program? What about all the ways you can spread the word about your business – social media, ads, blogging, podcasts – what do you do first?

This question – where do you start – quickly evolves into the next question – where do you focus?

As you start to see some success in your business, you get to the point where you simply don't have all the time and energy in the world to try out all the new ideas for growing your business. You realize time is one of your most valuable resources as an entrepreneur, *so you must invest your time wisely*.

But do you invest your time creating a new product or program?

Do you invest your time writing a new book?

Do you invest your time writing guest posts or getting interviewed or speaking?

If you've ever debated these questions *Where do I start?* or *Where should I focus?*, you aren't alone. Most entrepreneurs find themselves spinning their wheels for years, stuck in a business that just isn't growing, because they just aren't sure what to do next.

That's Where Your Business Sweet Spot Comes In.

When Francesca came to work with me in 2012, she was burning out. She realized current biz model was limiting her growth, but she just didn't know what to do next. After all, this current business was paying the bills and she couldn't just scrap everything and start from scratch!

Once we dove into her business, it became clear to me that she did not want to become the next rock-star yoga teacher gracing the cover of Yoga Journal Magazine. She had no desire stop working with her private clients completely to create an online business where she'd be spending more time in front of a screen than on a yoga mat.

Francesca adored being a private yoga

teacher! And after 10 years doing this work, had realized that her next step was being a teachers teacher, working closely with other yoga teachers to build the skills and confidence required for transformational private yoga lessons.

This was her Business Sweet Spot.

We just needed to realign her business to create more ease and less stress.

Simply knowing her Business Sweet Spot gave us the clarity we needed to quickly assess and take action in her business.

Her private yoga business was simplified by raising her rates and letting go of a few bad-fit clients. The results were immediate:: she maintained her level of income while reducing working hours.

And that was the opening she needed to develop the next stage of her business. Other yoga teachers had asked Francesca for years how she had built up such a successful private yoga business in one of the most competitive markets and she realized there was a major gap she could fill in the market.

Within a few months, she'd created a mentorship and private yoga teacher training program to teach other teachers how to confidently teach private yoga, all while creating the flexibility and freedom she craved for her life.

Your Business Sweet Spot Simplifies Your Business & Amplifies Your Results

When you understand your Business Sweet Spot, you have a framework to facilitate the decisions all entrepreneurs have to make.

> :: You'll understand how to design the RIGHT offerings for YOUR perfect-for-you clients {no more guessing – you'll have the tools to serve up EXACTLY what they want to get from you}.

:: You'll see how you NATURALLY attract community + clients {no more struggling to force yourself to follow some marketing or sales formula that just feels so inauthentic}

:: You'll stop struggling to make your business work {because it was custom tailored to work FOR YOU!}

We all want a business that allows us to create an amazing life {not just a living}.

A business that really works *for you* – a sustainable {profitable} business that allows you to share your greatest passion doing what you love with clients you adore.

After getting under the hood of thousands of businesses around the world, I know that for the majority of us this is the ultimate entrepreneurial dream.

Ready to turn this dream into your reality? This book will walk you through a process to discover your business sweet spot and create success on your own terms.

How to Use This Book

If you've ever found yourself spinning your wheels, asking questions like::

Where do I start?

What do I focus on first?

Which idea do I pursue next?

Rest assured that you're in the right place.

In the coming pages, you'll go on a journey to discover the best parts of yourself that are the building blocks for designing a business that you not only love, but that loves you back.

What is a business that loves you back?

When you design a business that loves you back, you're no longer attempting to squeeze your business into someone else's business model because you'll have a custom tailored strategy that highlights the best of what you bring to the table.

When you design a business that loves you back, you'll feel confident sharing your genius with the world without worrying that you're being pushy or salesy (in fact, marketing becomes more fun and effortless because it's simply an extension of what you're already doing in your business).

When you design a business that loves you back, you're building your business around your desired lifestyle. You're making time for work AND play. You're doing your business, your way.

And isn't that why we chose this lifestyle business anyhow? To have the freedom, ease, and abundance we all dream of so we can love every minute of this business and enjoy our lives? I think so!

In Part I, you'll explore why you must embrace not only your passion and your purpose in your business, but truly understand the people you are meant to serve to build a predictably profitable business. I'll walk you through a series of discovery exercises to laser in on each element of your Business Sweet Spot to help you create your own framework for strategic planning.

In Part II, you'll start by taking the Business Sweet Spot quiz to learn your primary Business Sweet Spot Theme. You'll receive a complimentary guide to your Business Sweet Spot Theme with an overview and next steps.

Finally, in Part III, you'll meet all four of the Business Sweet Spot Themes. You'll meet the creative Makers who adore rolling up their sleeves to bring a new idea to life. You'll hear from the charismatic Mavens who can inspire a movement with their message. You'll learn how essential Mentors are to facilitating transformation and change through their deep work with clients. And you'll see how strategic Masterminds uncomplicate the world around us by breaking down big challenges into step-by-step action plans.

This part of the book includes frameworks and strategies to help you unlock the power of your Business Sweet Spot in your business model for each stage of growth in your business.

With the strategies in this book, you'll have a clear framework to better evaluate what is, and isn't, working in your business so you can step into your role as CEO and confidently course correct to achieve your desired results.

You'll step into your 'Zone of Genius' where you are focusing your time and energy on growth strategies best suited to your strengths and personality instead of attempting to force a square peg into a round hole.

You'll learn how to harness your unique

Business Sweet Spot as your unique advantage, a key to standing out in a sea of others who do similar work with similar audiences.

This process isn't about drastically changing everything in your business – it's about identifying what is working for you and growing exponentially from there.

Ready to discover your Business Sweet Spot? Let's get started!

PART 1::
YOUR
BUSINESS
SWEET SPOT

Chapter 1:: Birth of The Business Sweet Spot

When you're trying to decide what kind of business to start, there are basically three distinct schools of thought::

1. Follow your passion and do what you love.
2. Focus on mastery of your greatest strengths and talents.
3. Go after the dolla dolla bills and do what it takes to make the moola.

The problem is, each of these ideas don't

work alone. And I speak from experience. I've tried all three!

As a college student, I was a music major with a focus in French Horn performance. Nothing made me happier than playing in orchestras and wind ensembles.

However, I quickly realized that I wasn't the most talented performer. In fact, I had to work much harder to even keep up with the top players. Eventually, all the hours of practicing solo in a 4×4 padded practice room led me completely resent what used to be a huge passion!

After two years struggling to keep up, I switched majors to Entrepreneurship and Small Business Management.

On the surface, made sense. With two entrepreneurial parents, I'd grown up working in the family business. I had a knack for numbers and marketing and by the time I was in graduate school, I was tutoring accounting, finance, and economics to undergrads. *I was also bored completely out of my mind.*

Then I was recruited straight out of my MBA program to go into financial and small business consulting. After all those years as a broke college student, the promise of a lucrative career was pretty damn enticing. So I went for it.

After just a few short years in that hyper-competitive world of 65+ hour work weeks, I started experiencing panic attacks and adrenal fatigue from a complete lack of self-care, extreme stress, and unhappiness.

Ten trips to the ER later, I took a medical leave of absence, jumped on a yoga mat and began my journey of self-discovery. Yoga became my tool for recovery and serendipitously became the next step in my career.

An opportunity came up to work with yoga apparel juggernaut lululemon athletica, so I moved to Vancouver, BC to immerse myself in all things yoga and lululemon as I was immersed in their culture and management training.

I was profoundly impacted by culture of personal development. It was through the lululemon's training program that I was first introduced to book *Good To Great* by Jim Collins.

Inside this book, he details the research he did to discover what it was that made some corporations really great and standout even in saturated markets. What was it that they did to grow leaps and bounds over the competition?

As he did this research, he created this framework called *The Hedgehog Concept*. The Hedgehog Concept takes three different areas of their business.

> *This is what every single great corporation has in common.*
>
> *They understand what they're deeply*

> passionate about, what they can be best in the world at and what drives their economic engine.
>
> The Hedgehog Concept is not about juggling a million balls in the air. It's not about getting distracted and chasing shiny objects.
>
> It's about narrowing down, having a core focus and being very deliberate with every single decision that you make so that you understand what your business really has to offer so you can make the right choices about what to put out into the world.

This framework asks three questions:: *What are you deeply passionate about? What can you be the best in the world at? What drives your economic engine?*

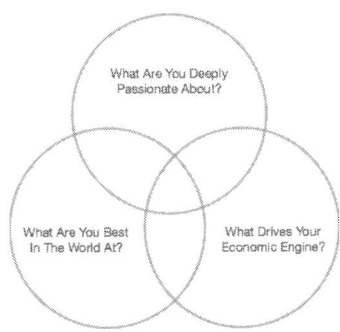

The most amazing part about lululemon

athletica is this company, as little as 10 years ago, they were an unknown brand. But when the founder Chip Wilson thought about what impact he wanted create in the world and how he wanted this business to take shape, he decided early on that their competition wasn't other small unknown brands in the fitness apparel space. They were looking at Nike. They were looking at Adidas. They were looking at major players in the space.

When they started looking at their competitive landscape, they decided the Hedgehog Concept would be the framework to determine their unique advantage.

What are you deeply passionate about? Helping people to become better athletes.

You only have to read the manifesto printed on every shopping bag to see lululemon's passion for helping people become better athletes. They are passionate about elevating the world from mediocrity to greatness. They want to give people the components they need to live happier, healthier lives. This is the WHY that drives their mission forward.

What can you be best in the world at? Women's black yoga pants.

You can't walk into a yoga or fitness studio without seeing women clad in the signature black lululemon yoga pants. Lululemon took a lot of time to make sure that they were really designing something that would become this cult classic in the yoga world. When they first introduced these pants, no other brands had the flat stitched seams, wide (flattering) waistbands, or sweat wicking material.

What drives your economic engine? Vertical Markets.

lululemon's meteoric rise to success, in a market already saturated by Nike and Adidas, was due to narrowly focusing in on their specific niche – yoga – and controlling the entire process from manufacturing to how they were sold.

By having their hands in every step of the process and serving an underserved niche of the athletic market, lululemon was able to become deeply entrenched in the rapidly growing yoga culture. In fact, I'd venture as far to say that lululemon was the catalyst for the major athe-leisure trend we see in mainstream fashion today (as I write this book while wearing my very comfortable and flattering yoga pants).

It's important to note that the entire hedgehog concept was designed not for solopreneurs and small business owners. It was designed based on researching huge, multi-million dollar corporations!

It's the intersection of these three questions that differentiates GREAT companies from the competition, however translating this to the world of heart-centered solo entrepreneurs requires some subtle shifts for this concept to become useful and applicable to your business strategy.

The Birth Of The Business Sweet Spot

The Business Sweet Spot was designed for solo entrepreneurs and small business owners who want to embrace the best of the Hedgehog Concept to simplify their business and amplify their results.

We'll start by honing in on your passion – your deeper WHY for this business you are building.

Then, we'll examine what you can be best in the world at – WHAT is your unique advantage.

Finally, we'll reveal your economic engine – HOW your business model generates predictable profits by designing offerings for your dream clients.

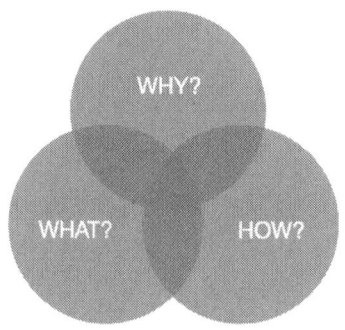

Once you discover your business sweet spot, you no longer have to force your business into success as it's now designed around what will make you the most successful.

Case Study:: Danielle LaPorte
Author of The Fire Starter Sessions and The Desire Map
Years ago, I ran into a blog post by Danielle LaPorte called *My Dominatrix of Decisions Rides a Hedgehog* that helped me to see how a personal brand could apply the Hedgehog Concept as a tool to stay focused when making big decisions in her business. **Danielle is deeply passionate about** *liberating truth.*

> *Freeing the truth and truth that frees. My purpose is to inspire authenticity – freeing talent, ideas, voice, opinions, consciousness. I journey to freedom. It's a cellular-level commitment, and when I've diverged from that path in the past, the cost has been dear. When I stay the course of my truth, and support others in doing the same, I prosper in every possible way.*

Danielle is best in the world at *sharing her journey via storytelling.*

> *Telling my story and inviting other people to relate. I racked my noggin' on this one. But eureka! It came to me...no one can tell my story or share my acumen like I can. My experience is what I sell and the more I show up, the better.*

Danielle's economic engine is *multimedia.*

> *I make money by packaging my wisdom in as many forms as possible, and most of those forms become passive income (ie. books.)*

For Danielle, multi-media experiences have been the

cornerstone of her business model. Her first book, The Fire Starter Sessions, were a $150 book with worksheets, downloadable audio, and video bonuses. Her books aren't just books. Danielle has built a business on digital experiences. She wants people to be able to not just read she's teaching but go even deeper with the material.

As we go through this process, you'll answer each of these questions for yourself. The pieces of the puzzle will start to come together as you go through the next few chapters.

Chapter 2:: Your Passion

Passion for your work is essential to having a thriving business.

Why?

Because passion is what helps you continue moving forward, even when you face the challenges of entrepreneurship.

If you don't have bigger reason WHY you are running this business, when you come up against those tough days or those slow periods when things just don't go as planned, it becomes much harder to dig in and keep going.

You have to have a deeper passion for what you do that keeps you inspired and committed to pursuing your vision.

Notice that we're not talking about your passion as if it's just the topic or hobby or interest you want to turn into a business. This is where so many get stuck when they start their entrepreneurial journey. They either have too many ideas they are trying to pursue all at once and nothing gets off the ground… or they simply change focus too quickly and never gain real momentum.

True passion is all about sharing your WHY – your bigger truth with the world.

As Simon Sinek shares in his amazing book *Start with Why*::

> "People don't buy WHAT you do, they buy WHY you do what you do."

Your passions – the interests and hobbies and topics you lose yourself in – are just the starting points that lead to a deeper WHY that helps you to stay inspired in your business as you inspire those around you.

Your WHY is essential to Your Business Sweet Spot as it sets your business apart from a sea similar businesses. While others focus the conversation on what they do or how they do it (all those very technical features), you are attracting and magnetizing your dream perfect-for-you clients by connecting to the deeper beliefs and values you share.

TOMS Shoes is a perfect example of a business with a clear passion. Technically, they are a shoe company. And every other shoe company in the world focuses on WHAT they do or HOW they do it. They focus on the fashion or the functionality of the shoe itself.

But while TOMS is now a household name, their messaging has nothing to do with the style of their slip-on shoes and has everything to do with their bigger mission to help those in need with their one for one initiative.

People didn't buy TOMS because of the shoes. They fell in love with the brand because of the PASSION behind the brand.

How can you tap into your passion and inspire others with your business?

CREATING YOUR PASSION STATEMENT

When you have a passion statement, you'll have a clear way to articulate what matters most, to you and your business.

Keep in mind that your passion statement might take a little while to create. It will always be a work in progress. In fact, you may find that as you continue sharing your WHY with others through your work, your passion becomes deeper and richer.

Once you have this core piece of your Business Sweet Spot figured out, you'll find that marketing becomes much, much easier.

You'll attract more clients by painting the picture of what's possible. You'll become more memorable and inspiring to your potential clients by connecting on a deeper level of shared values and beliefs.

In the following pages, you'll find some passion discovery questions to help you start the process of writing your own passion statement. Take these discussion questions to a quiet place where you can do some freestyle journaling or writing. Whether it's writing out full, freestyle sentences or just little notes and words to yourself, it's about teasing out your why – this bigger truth that you want to share with the world.

1:: What excites you most about your work?

What ideas or concepts or projects light you up? What motivates you to get up in the morning and get to work? What keeps you inspired to do your work each and every day? What are the things you can't wait to do?

What are you constantly drawn to and where you do spend your time? Why is that so amazing?

2:: If money was no object, what would you spend your time doing?

People are often asked this when they're approaching retirement. You might say they'd all say, *"I'm just going to sit on the beach and drink margaritas all day,"* but what really often happens is they might experience that version of retirement for a just a few months before they want to come back to work.

People want meaningful work. We have this innate desire to make a contribution; to make a difference. We want to be contributing to humanity to contribute to society in a meaningful way.

If your needs were met — if money wasn't the core reason you're creating a business — what would you really want to be doing?

What would be the most meaningful work for you? *Why is that so important to you?*

3:: If you could leave one piece of wisdom to your children, what would it be?

If you only were to leave one piece of wisdom for the next generation what would it be? Or imagine you were giving a speech to a room of graduating high school or college students. What would you tell them? What is the one thing you'd want them to know about you and what you stand for?

> **Draft your passion statement**
>
> Now review your answers and draft your first passion statement. Keep in mind, you want this to be about more than *I love teaching yoga and I want more people to do yoga* or *I love cooking and I want to share my love for food with other people.*
>
> It's about digging even deeper. What is it about yoga that you really love? What did it bring to your life that you want to share with others?
>
> A better passion statement could be *"I'm not just*

passionate about yoga, I'm passionate about helping other women feel incredibly confident and feel beautiful in their bodies, exactly as they are."

Do you see how much powerful that is? Digging deeper and continuing to ask why this is important will help you create a passion statement that naturally attracts and inspires others to your business.

Chapter 3:: Your Purpose

We often hear about discovering your life's purpose... but what about your business purpose?

In terms of the Hedgehog Concept, this is what your company can be the best in the world at.

As solopreneurs, can we really aspire to be the best in the world? That might set the standard so high that our perfectionism stops us from even trying! But we can bring our best to the world by turning our divine gifts into our unique advantage that helps you to stand out from the crowd.

Your divine gifts are this incredible combination of strengths, talents, life experience, education and skills that you have built and developed over your entire life.

It's not just about that one skill-set that we're kind of good at. It's not just about one talent you've had since childhood. It's about the combination of all of them. And when you bring this into your business, your set yourself apart.

> "There is a vitality, a life force, an energy, a quickening that is translated through you into action. And because there is only one of you in all of time, this expression is unique. And, if you block it, it will never exist through any other medium and will be lost." – Martha Graham

The purpose of your business is to bring the BEST of what you have to offer to the world! And you simply can't do that if you're stuck in your zone of competence or even your zone of excellence.

When you are in your Business Sweet Spot, your business is designed around what Gay Hendricks calls your Zone of Genius.

Your Zone of Genius is your one-of-a-kind divine gifts – those talents, skills, and experiences – that allow you to bring your best to your work. And even more fascinating, while you are in your Zone of Genius, you're more likely to enter a state of peak performance where your work leaves you feeling energized, in the flow, and reaching your full potential.

Operating in your Zone of Genius, in service to your PASSION aka your WHY, is the surest way to become known as the best in your field while also providing you, dear entrepreneur, with the most fulfillment and satisfaction in your work.

Almost ironically, the greatest barrier to leveraging your Zone of Genius is realizing that it is something that comes naturally to us. Most people don't even recognize their Zone of Genius so they spend more time pushing and trying to improve their weaknesses instead of discovering and honing their strengths.

Talk about forcing square peg in a round hole!

The entire world seems to focus on making everyone more well-rounded, but for entrepreneurs, attempting to be everything to everyone is a surefire way to eliminate your edge.

DISCOVER YOUR ZONE OF GENIUS

When you have a clearer understanding of your unique Zone of Genius, your business will have a clearer purpose focused on bringing the best of what you have to offer to the world!

Why? Because your divine gifts come more easily and naturally to you than they do to others. When you work on them just a little bit, when you practice them and refine them to get better at your craft, you will grow exponentially.

Comparatively, when you attempt to improve at your weaknesses, you'll only improve incrementally. You'll work much harder to improve on skills outside your Zone of Genius. You might become really good at them, maybe even excellent at them, but you'll never deliver your highest value to the world.

When you stand in your Zone of Genius, the rest of the world will have to hustle just to keep up with you! And that's an incredible unique advantage.

1:: Strengths Finder 2.0

This is hands down one of my favorite assessments to help you uncover your true strengths. The reason I believe so strongly in this specific assessment is it's not about how you view the world. *It's how you act in the world*. It's about how you manipulate the world around you; how you co-create with the world. Strengths are about how you approach your work.

When you take this assessment, you'll receive your top 5 strengths as well as receive a report about how you can leverage these more in your day-to-day. Sometimes the results may seem like a surprise but more often than not, they resonate deeply.

The insight I gained from learning my top 5 strengths – Input, Strategic, Learner, Maximizer, Intellection – helped me to see that my Zone of Genius would always be related to teaching and strategic planning. It also helped me to accept that some strengths I admire (and even wish I personally had), like Woo, just aren't in my Zone of Genius.

When you understand your strengths, you'll have a clearer picture of how you can best position yourself and your business by ensuring that your entire business strategy – from what you sell to how you market to designing your customer experience – is aligned with your strengths.

2:: Emailing Friends + Colleagues

This exercise isn't as scientific or precise as taking the Strengths Finder Assessment, but you will learn so much from those who you love and respect you about how they view you at your best.

Remember, we all naturally operate in these areas of strengths and, often, they come so easily and so effortlessly to us that we don't see that they're special. It's really only through these objective things – like taking a strengths finder or asking feedback from other people – that we actually see and appreciate our genius!

This is a straight-forward exercise to email 5-10 friends, family, colleagues, peers, former clients – anyone who has experience of working with you – and ask for their perspective on what you do best.

Send out individual emails to your list of trusted friends::

> Hey there,
>
> I'm hoping you'll take a few minutes to hit reply and help me out. I'm working on some elements of my business and would love an outsider's prospective on what I uniquely bring to the table. I'd so appreciate if you would take a few minutes and let me know what you feel are my best three strengths, talents or qualities. I deeply appreciate you taking the time to share this with me!

This might feel like a vulnerable exercise. I felt this way, too, the first time I reached out for feedback about the experience of working with me! But trust me once you do this, you will be so glad you did.

In fact, everyone I've ever assigned this to has come back to me saying, *"Oh, my gosh. I'm so glad I did this. It made me feel amazing to get all these incredible responses from my colleagues, clients and friends."*

If this is making you feel especially vulnerable, only send this exercise to people who feel SAFE to you – not people who you know are usually critical or quick to point out flaws. We are looking for what you do best!

Once you have these elements in place, you'll be able to start connecting the dots between your strengths finder and the replies you've gotten from your friends, family and colleagues.

> **Reflecting On Your Zone of Genius**
>
> **Do you feel like these answers are true for you?**
>
> What do you think about all the new insight you've received into what makes you special and different? I want you to think about a time that you've helped someone with these gifts. In fact, if you have a story about how you've helped them and what that process looked like, that's even better. That is GOLD for creating marketing that highlights your Business Sweet Spot.

> **When did you realize these gifts were special and not everyone else has them?**
>
> Did you have an inkling about this before we did the exercise? You probably have, so think about it. When did you realize these gifts were special? Do you have a story about that? Write a little bit about that as well. All of these elements are coming together and while you might not have a clear, concise summary yet, you're getting closer. I promise.

Remember, the purpose of your business is to highlight your unique divine gifts and zone of genius! After these exercises, you'll have some non-biased insight into what makes you unique. This is how we begin to differentiate you and your work from the 'competition.'

Get excited about the work that you've done so far. I know that this is deep work, but I promise all of these elements are going to be so essential and helpful as we pull together a strategy that feels authentic, like a true reflection of who you want to show up as in the world.

Chapter 4:: Your Prosperity Plan

Now we're filling in the third piece of the puzzle:: how do you generate predictable profits in your business?

This is the area in the original Hedgehog Concept that was called the Economic Engine. It is where the rubber meets the road. Once you understand this element of your Business Sweet Spot, you understand the profit model for your business. But, for heart-centered entrepreneurs, it's more than just how you make your money!

There are two key parts of the Prosperity Plan puzzle::

1. How we best serve our dream clients, and
2. What our dream clients *want from us* and *will happily pay for*!

Part 1 is understanding how we do our best work in the world. We've already talked about harnessing our passion and purpose in our Zone of Genius. Now it's time to package that up into a clear and compelling offering – a product, program, or service – that allows us to serve our clients while also allowing us to build a business that fits our overall business and lifestyle design plan.

Part 2 is listening, listening, listening to our dream clients to ensure our offerings are the perfect fit for what they want and need. This understanding of our dream clients will help us position our offerings so that our marketing attracts and resonates with those who will become our paying clients.

This is the heart of entrepreneurial alchemy. I love this quote from Dan Kennedy, one of the most respected copywriters out in the world today. He says:

> "What is entrepreneurship if not the conversion of your knowledge, talents and guts through the investment of your time into money?"

Let's do some entrepreneurial alchemy, shall we?

PART 1:: YOUR PROSPERITY PLAN

Let's start with the first piece of the prosperity plan puzzle – packaging up your zone of genius into a product, program, or service.

We want to look at your business from a really high level perspective. We're not diving into specific individual offerings here but we do want to determine HOW you deliver your core products, programs, or services. There are three primary ways you can deliver your offerings to your dream clients::

Done For You

Many service providers build their businesses around doing the work for their clients. This especially makes sense if the work to be done requires an expertise that they simply don't have and need to outsource to you for the best possible results or they simply don't have the time to accomplish this themselves.

Done for you services could be a fantastic option for you if your strengths lie in taking a project from idea to finished product. If you love to roll up your sleeves and handle all the details from start to finish, this is your sweet spot.

Examples of fantastic done-for-you service based businesses?

- Designing websites
- Creating meal plans and shopping lists
- Planning and organizing a wedding

But even if your business isn't a typical done-for-you service business, you may find that adding this aspect could set you apart! I love the example of a health coach who also creates customized nutrition and meal plans as a done-for-you version of their traditional coaching service.

Done With You

Many service providers have found that a done-with-you service is the best fit to help their clients achieve their goals. Often, they simply need the support and accountability of working with a professional.

Done With You could be an incredible fit for you if you are a people person who loves to be there with your clients, each step of the way. If you love helping people achieve their goals by holding them accountable and helping them through the ups and downs of a challenge, this could be your sweet spot.

Examples of great done-with-you service based businesses?

- Mentoring up and coming website designers
- Health and nutrition coaching
- Private yoga lessons

And even if your core business model isn't based on done-with-you services, you may find that adding this component could be an incredible game changer. For example, an online training program that offers additional one-on-one or group coaching can help students to ask questions and navigate roadblocks more easily to get the most from the program.

Done By You

If your experience and expertise lends itself to teaching others *How To*, then Done By You could be the perfect model for your business. Your clients feel confident that with the right training and education, they will be able to achieve their goal on their own.

Done By You generally makes a transition from services into products and programs. If you are a natural problem solver and organizer who likes to make sense out of all the information, then teach it step by step to others, this could be your sweet spot.

Examples of great done by you businesses?

- How to Build Your Website Training Program
- Everything You Need to Plan Your Wedding Workshop
- Virtual Yoga Studio Online Membership

The appeal of a done-for-you business lies in the potential for long term growth. Without needing to trade dollars for hours, you open up the opportunity to generate more leveraged or passive income. It quickly raises the number of people you can reach and impact through your work!

Nearly every business can gain the leverage and growth of a done-for-you product or program. For example, a website designer may create an online training program that teaches students how to create their own websites.

Next, we're diving into the second half of the prosperity plan puzzle – positioning your product, program or service so your dream client understands the value of what you are offering.

Then we can play matchmaker between the value that you can provide through your product, program, or service and the value that they are actively looking to buy.

UNDERSTANDING YOUR PEOPLE FIRST

The key to unlocking a profitable business starts with deeply understanding the people you are here to serve. *The most amazing part? When you focus on your people first... the profits naturally follow.*

Why are we talking about people first?

When you don't understand what your dream clients actually value (aka they will happily pay for), you have no business!

Understanding your people is an essential piece of designing a predictably profitable business. If we spend all of our time in our top-secret entrepreneur lab, getting so excited about our new ideas for products, programs, or services *without validating the ideas first*, you'll find that a lot of time and energy is wasted trying to create something people actually want to buy. You will struggle to get paying clients. You will have no business. There's no fuel going into that economic engine.

When you take the time to validate your ideas before developing your products, programs, or services::

You Meet People Where They Are.

Entrepreneurs often struggle from the curse of expertise – meaning we forget what it's like to be a beginner. The result? Our dream clients aren't sure if this offering is right for them or not! Often this is because we assume they know what we know.

For example, let's assume you have a dream client who wants to lose weight searching for a health coach. If she finds a health coach blog that is full on information on why you need a healthy gut, but doesn't actually talk about the relationship between gut health and trouble losing weight, she will assume she's in the wrong place. That coach isn't solving her perceived problem.

But if she stumbles on a health coach blog that is full of education that connects the dots between gut health and loosing weight, she's much more likely to take that next step towards working with that coach because she's been educated beyond the symptom she's struggling with and now sees the actual root cause of her problem.

You Learn Their Challenges.

Often people will come to you for help with with something they have already attempted to solve but they just can't overcome some roadblocks along the way. Sometimes is a lack of education for what the actual problem is. Sometimes it's self-sabotage. Sometimes it's lack of support. There are many reasons why people stumble and taking the time to validate your offering ensures that you can not only design a better offering but a better customer experience and better marketing copy to educate your dream clients.

You Prove You Can Get Results.

If you are offering your experience, expertise, and education in your business, then people want to know that your approach works. Validating your offering provides you with much needed proof that you are the real deal (and allows you to start building case studies and testimonials).

Once you've taken the time to understand the people you want to serve, you'll have a clearer idea of what value they place on your product, program, or service. Imagine how much more successful your content would be if you started from the perspective of your dream clients and spoke to their journey of trial and error!

Understand Your Dream Clients

For each offering, you'll want to answer each of these questions so you can more clearly articulate not only what your product, program, or service is about, but also why it's relevant and helpful to your dream clients.

What unique problem can I solve for my dream clients?

If your offering isn't solving a problem, consider what need or desire it is fulfilling.

What is their #1 struggle in solving this problem?

Often, they have attempted to solve this problem on their own. What roadblocks have they run into along this journey?

What specific results are they looking to achieve?

Get really clear here on not only what they want – but WHY.

If you are a weight loss coach, your client may want to lose 20lbs but really, she wants to look incredible in her wedding dress.

If you are a website designer, your client wants to professional website for her business, but really she wants to attract more high-end coaching clients.

What are people already ASKING me for help with?

Look for clues from your audience – sometimes a blog post with lots of shares or comments is a good indicator that people want more of that information from you. Double down on what works!

HOW do I want to deliver that product, program, or service?

What suits your Business Sweet Spot best – done with you, done for you, or done by you?

What could I provide that would take my business to the next level?

There are many options so consider carefully what would either allow you to achieve your business goals.

Chapter 5:: Articulating Your Business Sweet Spot

Now we will integrate everything that we've covered about so far in your Business Sweet Spot by bringing together all three of the core Sweet Spot elements: your passion, your purpose and your prosperity plan.

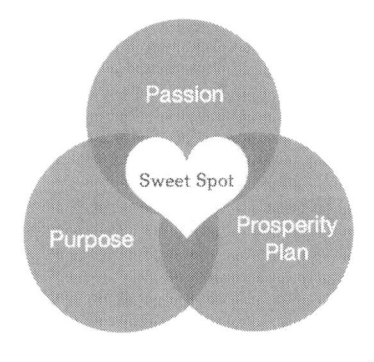

Passion / Purpose / Prosperity Plan / Sweet Spot

When you have a Business Sweet Spot that's

articulated in a clear, concise way, you can begin to use this as a filter for all the areas of your business:: from who you work with, to each offering that you put out into the world, to the way you use marketing to grow your business.

Our goal is to help you deeply resonate with your dream clients. This is what allows you to really stand apart from other people who might be doing similar work to you in the world.

PART 1:: YOUR PASSION

We've talked about the importance of not only having a passion, but a deeply WHY that drives your business. The next step is crafting a clear one or two line passion statement that becomes the central message you share through your business.

What do you believe about your work?

What is it that you're standing for?

What are you infusing through all of your business?

What is that key message that you want to leave the world with?

Let's review some examples based on heart-centered entrepreneurs I've personally worked with. You'll see how their passion statements tie in with other elements of their business Sweet Spot as well as how their entire Business Sweet Spot helps them to stand apart from others doing similar work.

Writer & Designer
Ready to change your life? Gratitude is the answer. I want to inspire millions to cultivate a daily gratitude practice to find greater health and happiness.

Life Coach
You are enough. You are worthy of your dreams. You are worthy of your desires. My

purpose is to help women become more precious to themselves.

Private Yoga Teacher

Real strength comes from living in the moment. My mission is to help people slow down so they can be more present and productive in their lives.

Health Coach

Life is happening right now. Embrace it. Don't wait until you're a size four to wear clothes you feel beautiful in, go dancing with your friends or have a romantic adventure. Live the life you've been dreaming of right now.

You can hear that these are powerful messages to get out into the world! It's messaging like this that helps to stand apart – because now you're driving a stake in the ground to claim *this is what I stand for, this is what I believe, this is why my work MATTERS.*

PART 2:: YOUR PURPOSE

This is your unique expression of divine gives that is only available in this universe through you. This is where we're tapping into your Zone of Genius – what you do better than most people while feeling incredibly fulfilled in your work.

We are answering that question we all dread... *"So, what do you do?"*

And we're transforming this from a simple statement of your job title to something that hints at the transformation you provide for your amazing clients.

I found that this little Mad Libs style statement is the easiest way to help you articulate what it is you do in a way that gets people curious to learn more!

I {do this type of work} for {this dream client} to {get this result}.

But, what I really do is... {paint the picture of the ultimate dream}.

My statement might sound something like:

> *I teach women entrepreneurs how to turn their passion into a predictably profitable business. But, what I really do is help them simplify, streamline, and systematize their business for more ease and less stress.*

Can you see how that answers both the superficial *"what I do"* statement plus a deeper transformational statement? It's about marrying those two together so that you clearly articulate your zone of genius. Let's look at some examples again.

Writer & Designer

I create inspirational journals, planners and card decks. But, what I really do is make it easy and beautiful for you to establish a daily gratitude practice.

Life Coach

I coach women who want to be happier with their life. But, what I really do is help women identify and break free from their inner critic who keeps self-sabotaging and holding her back.

Private Yoga Teacher

I teach private yoga to busy professionals and executives. But, what I really do is help them to create calm so they can be more present, powerful, and productive in their lives.

Health Coach

I'm an emotional eating coach for women who are ready to end the struggle with their weight. But, really, I inspire women to say YES to themselves and to life, 100% guilt-free.

You can start to hear how articulating your zone of genius is going to be hugely beneficial to you in your business. Not only as a tool that will help you create those magnetic marketing messages, but also to craft perfect offerings that your clients will love.

PART 3:: YOUR PROSPERITY PLAN

Finally, we're going to do some entrepreneurial alchemy to bring together your passion and your purpose in to the right prosperity plan for your business.

Once you have this piece, you can start to develop a business and marketing strategy that is 100% in alignment with your zone of genius – a strategy that helps you to package and position your secret sauce to set you apart from others in your industry.

Remember those two key pieces of the Prosperity Plan puzzle::

1. How we best serve our dream clients, and

2. What our dream clients *want from us* and *will happily pay for*!

At this stage of Your Business Sweet Spot, we are focused on your business model as a whole instead of specific offerings. We want to be focusing in on the *types* of products, programs, and services that make the most sense for your overall business strategy.

Using your notes from the last section, fill in this prosperity plan mad-libs::

My business thrives when I offer {This Type of Product/Program/Service} for {This Type of Client} so she can {have this results}.

My statement is:

> *My business thrives when I offer a online masterminds and business training programs for women entrepreneurs who are ready to grow their businesses, on their terms.*

This statement has become an essential element of my overall business design strategy. I'm not the best in the world (or the happiest) offering done-for-you services, but my zone of genius is aligned with teaching. My dream clients aren't looking for someone to step into the role as CEO of their business, but they are ready to learn how to think strategically as a CEO. When my business is focused on offering online masterminds and online training programs, I'm highlighting both how I work best and meeting the needs of my students!

Let's look at some examples again.

Writer & Designer
My business thrives when I create beautiful downloadable and print products such as journals and planners for women who want to include more gratitude and grace in their every day.

Life Coach

My business thrives when I offer live experiences, workshops, and group coaching programs for women who are ready to stop self-sabotaging and start reaching their highest potential.

Private Yoga Teacher

My business thrives when I bring private yoga sessions to the offices, gyms, and homes of busy professionals who need more calm in all the chaos.

Health Coach

My business thrives when I share my expertise and experience via multi-media, books, and self-study programs with women who want to feel empowered in their relationship with their bodies.

Having these three statements – Your Passion Statement, Your Purpose Statement, and Your Prosperity Plan – all help you by providing a clear framework and focus for your business strategy.

PART 2:: DISCOVER YOUR BUSINESS SWEET SPOT

What Is Your Business Sweet Spot Theme?

Too often, entrepreneurs find themselves adopting the strategies of what worked for someone else without thinking if those strategies are really in alignment with their Zone of Genius. That's like putting on someone else's dress and hoping that you're exactly the same height, weight, and bra size.

Why wear someone else's strategy when you can custom tailor a strategy to fit you and your business?

That's where the Business Sweet Spot Themes come in.

After years of teaching the Business Sweet

Spot, I realized my students started to fall into four distinct camps. Some did really well with more high-touch, referral based business strategies. Others did incredibly well tapping into the high-tech online marketing scene. I took note of what was working best for different entreprenuers... then 5 years later, I created the Business Sweet Spot Themes.

I call these themes:: The Maker. The Maven. The Mentor. The Mastermind.

Once you're able to unlock your Business Sweet Spot Theme, it can ensure that your business and marketing strategy really works *for you.*

TAKE THE QUIZ TO DISCOVER YOUR BUSINESS SWEET SPOT THEME
HTTP://WWW.RACHEALCOOK.COM/QUIZ/

Once you answer a few short questions *based on what you do best,* you will discover if your Business Sweet Spot is as a Maker, a Maven, a Mentor, or a Mastermind. You will also receive a *Business Sweet Spot Inspired Action Guide* that is based on your theme with key insights and inspired action steps to grow your business.

After you have completed the quiz and have your Business Sweet Spot Theme results, you can review the theme descriptions found in Part III of this book. Each of these theme descriptions will help you to understand how your Business Sweet Spot Theme plays out in your unique business.

For each of these themes, this section shares a theme overview, case studies, and strategies that align best with your unique Business Sweet Spot.

Remember, the goal of Your Business Sweet Spot is not to provide a cookie-cutter one-size-fits all business blueprint – it simply helps you to find your greatest opportunities for growth as you apply more focus to your business strategy.

PART 3:: ALIGNING WITH YOUR SWEET SPOT

Maker

Lysa Greer took the leap into entrepreneurship after being laid off from her job of 12 years working behind the scenes in a media company on radio production and marketing campaigns.

Prior to being laid off, she had started freelancing on the side working on websites and social media for small businesses. While she had a small severance to tide her over for a month or two, as a single mom she needed stability and cash flow, stat.

She applied to job after job, but not one called back for an interview. Meanwhile, her four freelance clients started sending referral after referral. Lysa took it as a sign that she was meant to get serious in her business and turn her experience and skills into a service.

As she immersed herself into the world of online entrepreneurship, Lysa quickly realized that as a Maker with a hint of Mentor, she had more to offer than a typical $20 an hour virtual assistant. She could coach them through big decisions required to map out every step of a strategic plan to make their vision a reality.

She repositioned her services as an experienced expert instead of a task taker, which allowed her to not only quickly triple her rates, but become more selective about who and how she wanted to serve. With this clarity, Lysa designed her business for the freedom and flexibility she craved.

ARE YOU A MAKER?

If Lysa's story sounds familiar, your Business Sweet Spot lies in making dreams a reality. Makers are the doers of the world. As a

Maker, you lead by implementing and seeing the project through from start to finish. You know how to make things happen. Where others are dreamers – you are a DOER.

You love tackling big complex ideas and bringing order to chaos. While many Makers are drawn to creative pursuits such as design, writing, or photography, there are many who bring creative processes and problem solving to help others behind the scenes in their life or business (think of a wedding planner or a project manager).

Makers are the practitioners of the world. They not only see the vision, they see how they can bring together all the pieces of the puzzle and present the final product.

WE WANT YOU TO BRING OUR DREAMS TO LIFE

People reach out to Makers to tap into your innate creativity and talent. You are a master at your craft (that's right – you've got mad skills!) honed over years of doing the work. Your clients know that with your experience and expertise, you will help them get the best results possible.

Sure, we could attempt to learn how to take our own photos... or we could take a stab at designing our website... but at some point, we realize the incredible value of having a talented professional. When we want something done, and we want it done right, we turn to you.

Of all of the Sweet Spot Themes, the Maker is most likely to *do for us*. Once you understand the vision, you take the project off our plate and work your magic. As a Maker, you're naturally wired to taking full ownership of a project from start to finish. You love to be involved in each step of the process (either doing the work or managing those doing it) to ensure your standards are being met.

MAKER STRENGTHS

1:: Creativity

When someone shares a big idea, you love brainstorming all the ways to bring it to life. Nothing gets you more excited than diving right into the creative process and creating inspiration boards. Once you get a feel for the direction of the project from your client, you can start narrowing your focus and editing down to the most essential elements for any project.

Creativity isn't just about the big picture ideas either – it's about being able to navigate the project through all the ups and downs. Makers learn to confidently make the call on all the nitty gritty details and decisions that must be made from start to finish.

2:: Expertise

We come to you when we want the absolute BEST, highest quality result possible. The most successful Makers understand that to be the best in your field, you have to dedicate yourself to deliberate practice and mastery of your craft.

In Malcolm Gladwell's Outliers, his research shares that it takes 10,000 hours of deliberate practice to become a master at any skill. The most successful Makers haven't become successful overnight. While they all are incredibly talented, their journey to success came after years of consistently honing their skills and doing the work.

3:: Follow-Through

Chances are, you love to see projects through from ideation to implementation. Whether leading a team or implementing solo, you move us to the finish line.

However – you may suffer from *cobblers children have no shoes syndrome* when it comes to implementing for your own business. Make sure your business is as high on your priority list as your clients!

MAKER STRUGGLES

1:: Trading Dollars for Hours

Many Makers struggle to grow their business beyond done-for-you services or highly-custom products. Before you can grow your Maker business with leveraged or passive products, programs, or productized services, you've got to find a way to create a clear process for your work.

Some creative Makers struggle with the idea of systems and structure, but this is the secret to better managing your high-end custom work and creates a foundation for future growth. Simply starting by documenting your creative process can help pave the way for productized services, bringing on team members, or even teaching others how to do what you do.

2:: Marketing

While it is possible to build a Maker business based on referrals and word-of-mouth, growing your business to predictable profits requires consistent strategic marketing.

Look for opportunities to showcase your amazing creative work and clients! Thanks to the popularity of highly visual social media, it's easier than ever to give a peek behind the scenes or show off your best work and attract more amazing clients into your business.

3:: Boundaries

Because of the high-touch nature of your work, Makers often struggle with scope-creep or clients who demand more than initially agreed.

Start with clear contracts and expectations set up front, with a clear on-boarding process for new clients that helps them learn at the start of a project exactly how to communicate with you. Remember that managing client expectations is a big part of the job, and the more proactive you are, the more your clients will rest easy that the project is in good hands.

MAKER PROSPERITY PLAN

Most Makers start their entrepreneurial journey as freelancers, however shifting from a freelancer model to a more sustainable (and financially stable) business model requires moving beyond some more strategic planning.

Makers do well taking on freelance projects as the fastest path to building a profitable business during the startup stage of their business. Avoid the common trap of trading dollars-for-hours and start looking at how you can position your services based on projects (such as a new website) or packages (such as writing 20 social media posts plus providing graphics). This focus on the outcome helps you to price based on the value you offer instead of the hours you've worked.

As you gain experience, a productized service can help you to create even more leverage in your business. This takes the creative process you've likely honed offering custom work for hire and streamlines it into a package that can be offered to a wider range of clients for a standard price point.

If you prefer to work longer term with a smaller pool of clients (smart move for you, Maker!), consider creating a retainer or lifecycle business model that allows your former clients to continue working with you long term.

For example, 1) in a retainer business model, once a website design is completed, the designer may offer to work on a retainer that includes graphics for monthly blog and social media posts or 2) if the designer only wants to work on bigger projects, they might continue to nurture that same client to gain additional website projects such as sales pages, event pages, or website updates in the coming year.

Ready to scale your Maker business? Many business models can be built on a signature process. If you are confident delegating and managing projects, you may consider hiring other Makers to implement the work as you focus on the higher level strategy and direction. If you love to teach others, you may enjoy turning your signature process into a class or workshop. Or maybe you enjoy helping others in your field? You might be a natural mentor and coach for up and comers!

As a Maker, consider that your business strategy is centered around one core purpose:: turning your creative process into a high-touch boutique-style business.

MARKETING FOR MAKERS

As a Maker, your work is unique in that you truly do not need many clients to create a profitable sustainable business! However, for long term profitability and sustainability, you'll want to create a solid marketing strategy with a clear focus on bringing in rave reviews, referrals, and repeat business.

In Sweet Spot Strategy, we design your entire marketing strategy around the customer journey – the process we take people through to help them move from simply being aware we exist to building trust and relationship to inviting them to work with us.

Based on the consumer psychology of buyer readiness, this process helps ensure that your marketing system is continuously moving people through the journey, step by step.

Customer Journey

Attract → Engage → Nurture → Invite → Delight

The core stages of the Customer Journey include::

Stage 1:: Attract

These are the marketing strategies you likely think of when it comes to gaining exposure for your business – however as a Maker, you'll likely find that the best strategies are more boutique than mass marketing. Attract strategies that align best with Makers include building relationships with other connectors and influencers to create a network of referral sources and opportunities to showcase your work for their communities.

Referral Partners:: As you begin building your business, keep your eyes out for niche mates who offer complimentary products, programs, or services that your dream clients are already using. For example, if you are a wedding planner, get to know wedding photographers, wedding venues, and wedding dress shops.

You may even offer a referral fee to those partners, or have a special package only available for their clients. When you consider the higher end work you offer, a great referral partner could be responsible for thousands of dollars in revenue. Take amazing care of these partners!

Referral Events:: Remember, as a Maker, your job is to showcase your work to the right audience. You may throw a co-hosted event with another business, or simply participate by donating your products or gift card for your services as a potential door prize. Get engaged and involved with other entrepreneurs in your niche to create more opportunities for live events.

Press Coverage:: This may not apply to all Makers, but the higher end your services, the more you may want to look into getting featured in industry magazines and nominated for industry awards. This will help to not only get more eyes on your work, but give another layer of prestige and authority to your brand.

Stage 2::: Engage

Most Makers don't need access to thousands of generic contacts – they need a carefully curated database of the *right* contacts. This database should include all your clients and potential clients as well as your niche mates and referral partners.

As people begin to interact with your business, you'll want to add these potential clients to your database as well. The most important piece of contact information for potential clients? Hands down – their email address. Email is the easiest, cheapest, most convenient way for you to nurture those relationships so when a potential client is ready to take the next step, you are the first person they think of.

You'll also want to keep more detailed records as people become more engaged with your business so you can offer more high-touch communication with a personalized touch.

Stage 3:: Nurture

Once someone gives permission for you to contact them {preferably via email, then phone and mailing address}, it's up to you to stay top of mind. That's where Nurture marketing comes in. This is where you showcase your amazing clients!

As a Maker, each time you share what you've created for your clients, you give them an opportunity to shine. Keep in mind that your clients likely know another 3-5 potential dream clients who are also searching for your services... so while most of the people who are liking their wedding photos are just friends and family, a select handful are also newly engaged brides who are hunting for a wedding photographer. Make it easy for them to share and show off your fantastic work!

Social Media:: Can you showcase your work in a visual way? Nearly all social media is moving towards a visual platform. Share peeks into the behind the scenes of your creative process via Snapchat. Showcase your latest work {and tag your clients} for maximum shares on Facebook. Give inspiration for potential clients to pin to their dream boards on Pinterest.

Blog:: You might wonder if blogging applies to your business – but again, if your work is something your dream clients aspire to have, blogging is a fantastic platform to share the highlights behind the scenes, give a peek into the creative process, or even simply share the gorgeous final results.

Email:: A newsletter may, or may not, make sense for your business depending on the lifecycle of your clients. For example – if you are in the wedding industry, you might nurture potential clients with an automated email sequence starting the date they signed up for your free planning checklist… but they will likely be uninterested in 6-12 months to hear about your services. But a website designer might be able to offer regular insights into website design trends, showcase new work, and relay announcements for available openings.

For Maker, your email strategy may be a hybrid of a mass newsletter and high-touch individual emails to potential clients.

Stage 4:: Invite

When it comes to higher-end custom services, for Makers, you'll likely need to have a clear invitation strategy that walks people through the process of working with you and sets the expectations up front for the most enjoyable experience.

There is no need to become a pushy-sales person in order to have invitation conversations with potential clients! You'll simply want to have a clear agenda that helps you to navigate the conversation without finding yourself grasping for words or feeling under.

Be as prepared as possible for these conversations! Be ready with not only examples of your work, but also a clear step-by-step explanation of how you work so your clients start with clear boundaries in place.

Stage 5:: Delight

This is the stage where most stop thinking about marketing – but when you design and deliver an incredible customer experience, you'll see more rave reviews, referrals, and repeat business. Makers who spend time designing an incredible experience, from start to finish and beyond, often see a return of investment for years to come.

Impeccable Customer Experience. If you want not only happy clients, but long term clients who rave about you to their friends, family, and colleagues, experience is essential. A fantastic experience isn't just about fun gifts – it's all about clear communication, expectations, and anticipating the needs of your clients. This is where you not just do what you were hired to do – but go the extra mile. The more your clients feel like you're fully in control and understand their needs, the happier they will be.

Referrals. Referrals are everything. EVERYTHING! Especially for Makers. Referrals allow you to focus on what you do best and build a solid reputation. These can come from clients or referral partners, however sitting back and waiting for referrals to come your way isn't going to cut it. You've got to ASK for the referrals. Make a plan to followup with all your clients, host client appreciation events, and offer incentives for your best referring clients.

Rave Reviews. Why do we know the most amazing copywriters or designers or photographers {or insert any other makers here}? Because they focus on their clients first. They make their clients look like rockstars. This works especially well when you can use visual storytelling or share clear before + afters {for example, an amazing interior designer will have you drooling over the photos of her clients new homes}. Sharing those aspirational images {or telling the story of your clients or even better –

both!} will go a long way in people believing you can do the same for them.

Maven

When Casey Berglund decided to pursue her passion for health and nutrition, she knew her path was bigger than earning her degree in nutrition and food science then working in the healthcare field as a staff nutritionist.

She had experienced her own deep transformation and growth with her relationship to food, she realized that the traditional approach to nutrition just wasn't working for people most. We constantly hear the same information on healthy eating over and over – and still, the vast majority of adults struggle with their health.

Realizing the impact of her yoga and mindfulness practice on her eating habits,

Casey made it her mission to share a new approach to food and health that wasn't about diets or deprivation but instead was based on mindfulness and evidence-based nutrition.

A natural Maven, Casey looked for opportunities to share her message *"Ditch the All or None:: Eat for Fuel Flavor & Fun"* as a speaker and contributor. In addition to regularly speaking at conferences and events, she quickly became a National Spokesperson for Dietitians of Canada, a regular guest expert on the morning news show Global Calgary, and contributor for Canadian Living and Huffington Post.

ARE YOU A MAVEN?

If you are like Casey, your Business Sweet Spot lies in *inspiring others.* Nothing excites you more than exciting others around the possibility of big, life-changing ideas. Combined with their natural charisma and presence, Mavens are the speakers and leaders we turn to for inspiration.

As a natural leader, you love to rally people around a cause. Your natural charisma helps you to effortlessly attract and grow a community of people who look to you for fresh ideas and new approaches. You've likely held leadership positions in the past where you've inspired and motivated the team to take action towards a new and exciting future.

You have a magnetic presence that refuses to be hidden away as a best kept secret. Where others shy away from public speaking, you jump at the opportunity to share your message across all mediums. You enthusiasm and confidence makes you a natural speaking on stage at a conference or presenting as an expert on the news.

Mavens are the catalysts of the world. They see opportunities and adore big out-of-the-box ideas that have the potential to revolutionize the way we approach life, health, relationships, spirituality, and business.

WE WANT YOU TO INSPIRE US

We look to Mavens for inspiration and motivation. We listen to your podcasts on our daily commute to bring a boost of positivity to our day. We tune into your YouTube channel for your weekly show. When we hear that you are hosting a live event, we are the first in line for tickets.

It was no mistake that you are called a Maven. After all, a Maven is an expert, an aficionado, a connoisseur. You are the trendsetter we aspire to become in our lives, our health, and our relationships. You lead us into the future of new possibilities.

MAVEN STRENGTHS

1:: Presence

You might be charming. You might be

commanding. One thing is for sure – you definitely attract people to you *with ease*. This is possibly your greatest asset as you leverage your Maven Sweet Spot.

Mavens do exceptionally well as speakers and presenters. Of all the Business Sweet Spot Themes, Mavens tend to feel the most comfortable and confident in front of an audience. From speaking at in-person live events to getting interviewed on podcasts, many Mavens find that sharing their message through speaking is a powerful way to attract their tribe.

2:: Leadership

We come to you when we are ready to move into action. Your dream clients look to you for the inspiration and motivation to get into action.

To leverage this Maven strength, keep in mind that your role is as the catalyst, not the cheerleader. While you ignite the spark and excitement in others, your natural strengths are in the bigger picture more than handholding individuals through the every single baby step.

3:: Ideas

You love big ideas. But the key to a successful Maven platform isn't to re-hash the same old, same old. Like a fashion designer, you easily see how you can put a new spin on a big idea to make it exciting, modern, and new.

A word of caution – your excitement can feel like hype to others. Make sure you have a proven track record with your ideas so you don't come across as *All Sizzle and No Steak*.

MAVEN STRUGGLES

1:: Idea Overload.

Many Mavens get excited by so many amazing ideas to the point that they struggle to stick with one long enough to gain real momentum in your biz.

Avoid letting too many ideas turn into distractions by creating a clear container for your message. For example, under Casey's message of *Fuel, Flavor, and Fun*, you'll find articles and videos about recipes, body positivity, and mindfulness. All her content reinforces her message and positions her as an expert.

2:: Experience.

Mavens are excited about building an audience… but don't forget to get real experience delivering results first!

This means getting results for more than just yourself. It means working through your ideas with lots of people – 1×1 or in groups – before you attempt to scale your business via huge online courses or big events. Not only will the experience help ensure your content delivers results, but you'll build a solid base of raving fans who share their experiences and testimonials.

3:: Consistency.

Mavens tend to struggle the most with consistently implementing a plan *(because all the ideas!!!)* – but this is exactly what will help nurture and grow an audience over the long haul.

The secret to consistency in your marketing strategy is all about systems. When you have a clear process in place, you can more easily do the fun creative work when you are most inspired then share that content over a longer period of time.

MAVEN PROSPERITY PLAN

Many mavens do extremely well by building large platforms and audiences around their big idea. The more ways you can get your message into the world, the faster your business will grow.

However… you can't skip over building a solid foundation for your business!

For most Mavens, this starts with a single

focused idea that becomes the foundation for a signature product or program. As you work through your material with individuals or small groups, you'll have the opportunity to understand what motivates as well as what slows down the process.

As you design your signature offering, leverage your Maven strengths for an experience that transforms people's lives. Where others lecture or teach step by step, focus your energy on engaging through storytelling, insightful questions, and experiential exercises that go straight to the heart of your clients.

As you refine your signature product or program, you'll not only establish your expertise and experience but lay the foundation for a much bigger platform that has the potential to inspire thousands of people. What starts as a humble 10 person workshop hosted in someone's living room can quickly grow to into live events with hundreds of attendees when you have a solid message and powerful process to guide people through.

There are many opportunities to leverage your signature product or program::

- Information Products (such as Books, DVDs, CDs)
- Online Courses
- Keynote Speaker
- Live Events
- Conferences
- High-End Coaching or Masterminds
- Certification or Train the Trainer Programs
- Licensing Programs

As a Maven, consider your business a multi-media platform that serves one purpose:: getting your message out into the world!

MARKETING FOR MAVENS

It's one thing to build a community of raving

fans, it's another to convert those fans into happily paying customers! That's where a solid marketing strategy is essential for Mavens.

In Sweet Spot Strategy, we design your entire marketing strategy around the customer journey – the process we take people through to help them move from simply being aware we exist to building trust and relationship to inviting them to work with us.

Based on the consumer psychology of buyer readiness, this process helps ensure that your marketing system is continuously moving people through the journey, step by step.

Customer Journey

Attract → Engage → Nurture → Invite → Delight

The core stages of the Customer Journey include::

Stage 1:: Attract

These are the marketing activities that help you bring awareness of you, your brand, and your message to new audiences. Attract strategies include interviews, public speaking, and networking. Mavens *adore* attract marketing strategies because this is likely where you shine the most!

Speaking & Interviews:: The secret to getting more speaking & interview opportunities? Not waiting for them to come to you! If you want to have more opportunities to get your message in front of established audiences {a smart move for you, Maven!}, then develop a process to consistently pitch yourself. It does take some trial and error, but as you experience under your belt, you'll find opportunities will come to you!

Networking:: Ever heard the saying – it's not WHAT you know but WHO you know? As a Maven, you are likely building your network without even meaning to! Start being more intentional about the events you choose to attend (and if you aren't attending live events – even as an attendee you will meet incredible people who may become clients or important contacts) and consistently followup with people who you meet.

Stage 2:: Engage

This stage is where those new audiences essentially raise their hand and let you know they are interested in learning more (this permission is given when they visit your website and join your email list, or follow a social media channel).

As a savvy Maven, keep your eye on the long-term picture of building your business. Social media trends come and go very quickly but your email list is an asset that can strategically grow your business. Use your social media channels to connect and inspire, then direct them back to your online hub to build your email list with an incentive of a free video or audio.

Stage 3:: Nurture

The majority of the relationship building is done in this stage of the Customer Journey. This is where you give, give, give lots of inspirational, motivating content that highlights your natural charisma and presence. Mavens do extremely well with audio or video platforms such as podcast or video. Remember, your people want to see and hear you!

Consistency is the key for a successful content marketing strategy, but this may not be a strength. The most successful Mavens learn to batch create a lot of content at once, then schedule it's release over time. This helps capitalize on your creative highs while appearing consistent to build that know, like, and trust factor quickly.

Podcasts:: If your audience is on the go,

podcasts could be a fantastic option. People love that they can listen to podcasts in the car, at the gym, or cleaning up after dinner. Podcasts can have a range of show formats – from solo shows where you discuss a single topic to inviting a co-host to talk with you to interviewing guests – there is a lot of variety available for you.

Video:: If your audience would get the most out of seeing you do something, video is an amazing way to stand out. A quick search through YouTube shows that people are searching for makeup tutorials, fitness routines, and more. The cost of producing great video has come down dramatically – these days, you can record HD video with nothing more than your iPhone.

Stage 4:: Invite

You have to actually invite people to take that next step and pay for your products, programs, and services. For Mavens, this often means having a clear launch strategy that builds excitement and anticipation for your offerings.

Challenges:: Want a fun way to motivate and inspire people by helping them achieve a small win in their life, health, or relationships? Run a challenge! Challenges can be a fantastic way to quickly build your list with interested potential clients and give them a sample of what they would experience inside your offering.

Livestream Launch Party:: Why have a webinar when you can instead host a live-streaming launch party? This allows you to showcase your Maven strengths by allowing people to connect with you virtually as you share key insights and preview your offering.

Video Series:: If you've watched a traditional online launch strategy, you've seen a three-part video series or two. These can be a powerful way to introduce people to a new way of thinking and get them excited to take the next step with you.

Stage 5:: Delight

Once someone has purchased your book, joined your program, or attended your live event... then what?

Delight is all about surprising and delighting your clients by providing an amazing customer experience that has those people coming back for more. While many Mavens focus on attracting as many people as possible into their businesses, it's important to keep in mind that it's 7X more expensive to attract a new client than to keep an existing one!

Design your offerings with a stellar experience so they don't collect dust on the virtual shelf. When you take the time to engage your clients, not only will you see more amazing results from your students, but those students will continue coming back to you for higher level programs and services.

Mentor

After several years working as a social worker, Heather was unhappy, unfulfilled, and burned out. She was a working mama with two young boys who wanted to live an incredible life but wasn't sure exactly how she could leave the traditional career path to pursue her passion for teaching mindfulness and meditation to children.

Her own son had seen dramatic improvements in his focus and attention thanks to these practices, and before long, Heather was sharing with other parents who were struggling with their kids.

As she was searching for answers on starting a business, she came across information about turning your passion into a profitable online business. But the typical expert advice just wasn't a perfect fit for Heather's personality.

While she craved the freedom and flexibility of an online business, she didn't love sitting in front of her computer 7 days a week! In fact, she loved talking to her clients to see amazing breakthroughs. She loved teaching in person workshops and events. She craved connection.

Once Heather had that clarity, she was able to design a hybrid business that allowed her the freedom and flexibility to provide deeply transformational coaching via Skype to parents around the world while still offering the high-touch connection she craved with her clients in person and on retreats.

ARE YOU A MENTOR?

If Heather's story sounds similar, chances are your Business Sweet Spot lies in empowering and encouraging others. Mentors are the cheerleaders of the world. As a Mentor, you lead through relationship building. Driven by connection, you are the glue that holds the group together and the one we turn to when we need encouragement, support, and accountability.

Your ability to connect and build real relationships is one of your greatest strengths. Unlike other sweet spot themes, your natural understanding of others allows you to develop the trust required to facilitate meaningful change and deep transformation in the lives of your clients and community.

You have a positive and nurturing presence that makes you a people-person. Relationships are essential to Mentors! You have a deep need to feel connected to your community in order to feel fulfilled by your work. The minute that you feel too distanced from your clients or your community, it stops feeling good.

Mentors are the natural cheerleaders of the world. They see the potential in everyone and work side-by-side to help us achieve our goals in life, health, relationships, spirituality, and business.

WE WANT YOU TO HOLD OUR HAND

We seek out Mentors when they are ready for real change, but know we can't do it without real support and accountability. Often, we have attempted this journey by ourselves but ran into self-sabotage or confusion. We look to you to help us do what we can't do alone.

Of all of the Sweet Spot Themes, the mentor is the most hands-on. You are working right there side by side with those clients. You are encouraging and empowering them each step of the way. You are providing that support and accountability to help them navigate the obstacles and the inevitable self-sabotage. When they fall down, when they get discouraged, you are there to keep them moving forward.

You are the Yoda to our Luke Skywalker. A Mentor is a trusted advisor and guide to knows the journey ahead. You see our potential, guiding us step by step to reach it. You know that our obstacles to success often require facing our demons – and you're there to help us continue moving forward when it gets tough.

MENTOR STRENGTHS

1:: Connection

You might have a large circle of friends or a handful of close confidants, but you effortlessly build meaningful relationships with others. This is your greatest asset as you align with your Mentor Sweet Spot.

The power of connection drives your business forward. Of all the Sweet Spot Themes, Mentors have a tendency to grow their business very intuitively and organically when they focus on building relationships with potential collaborators and community.

2:: Community

You have a knack for bringing people together. From dinner parties to workshops, you have an intuitive sense of who would get along.

This talent for making introductions and creating community serves Mentors not only as they grow their community, but as they facilitate groups of people working to achieve similar goals. As you grow your business, this presents an opportunity to create more leverage by offering group programs, workshops, and retreats.

3:: Transformation

When you work with your clients, you go DEEP. You're not afraid to dig right into their challenges to help them get to the other side.

A note of caution – change is hard for everyone. It's especially hard when your clients have struggled for years with the same challenge. It's important that your clients are coachable and accepting personal responsibility... remember at the end of the day, it's up to them do the work.

MENTOR STRUGGLES

1:: Saying YES

Many Mentors are natural people pleasers who say yes to everything, leading to burnout, resentment, and frustration. Say YES to yourself first. If you want to deeply serve others, you've got to make sure you have the boundaries and structure in place to take care of yourself.

Your dream clients look to you for structure and support. You've got to make sure you've clearly defined how you work and who you serve to attract the right people while avoiding burnout.

2:: Niching Down

Mentors want to help everyone! But when it comes to differentiating yourself and your business, a clearly defined niche is crucial.

How can you define your niche? Start with the problem you are here to solve. If you can clearly articulate the challenge your dream clients are struggling with, they will more clearly see the value you provide.

3:: Feast or Famine

Without the right offerings and strategy in place, Mentors often find themselves hustling to bring in clients or get existing clients to commit long term.

Meaningful change rarely happens in a single one time session. As a Mentor, you serve best by helping your clients through the entire journey. Map out that journey so you can stop selling one-off sessions and start taking your clients from start to finish.

MENTOR PROSPERITY PLAN

Most Mentors spend their careers happily building intimate communities over huge faceless audiences. Because you are wired for meaningful connection, you'll find long term success building a solid client base that you serve long-term.

While many Mentors absolutely love working individually with clients, they often struggle to make the grow their business beyond working one-on-one. While trading dollars for hours can be a great start for your business, it often is unsustainable over the long term.

The first step out of the dollars for hours trap is moving away from single sessions and designing packages for your clients. Build your packages based on what will best help your clients to achieve their goals instead of an arbitrary number of sessions. Does it take 3 months for them to make that lifestyle change a habit? 6 months to get in the best shape of their life for their first fitness competition? Positioning your offerings based on results is the best way to command higher rates and build a solid foundation for your business.

As you continue working with your private clients, think about the next steps on their journey with you. While many clients may continue working with you in the same one on one format, many may be interested in higher level experiences such as VIP days, retreats, or group coaching.

As you design your signature offerings, leverage your Mentor strengths to facilitate meaningful change through empowerment and encouragement. Where others leave us to figure out the nitty gritty details, you can build in opportunities via live calls to ask questions, determine limiting beliefs, and break through resistance. A higher touch approach to your offerings help your clients to get even better results.

Hybrid programs can be a huge opportunity

for Mentors who are ready to reach and serve more people. If you've been interested in the leverage of creating an online program, but you want to maintain that connection and relationship with your clients, a hybrid program allows you to bring the best of both worlds to your work. By adding in additional levels of support – ranging from an online group to group calls to one-on-one work – you'll be able to give people the access they need to achieve their best results.

There are many opportunities to leverage your signature product or program::

- Information Products (Books, DVDs, CDs)
- Group Coaching Programs
- Live Events
- Retreats
- Immersions
- High-End Coaching or Masterminds
- Certification or Train the Trainer Programs

- Licensing Programs

As a Mentor, consider your business a relationship-centered community that serves one purpose:: building trust through connection!

MARKETING FOR MENTORS

While it's possible to build a Mentor business completely via word of mouth, you'll experience more consistent clients and cash flow when a clear marketing strategy is designed to bring in referrals and repeat business.

In Sweet Spot Strategy, we design your entire marketing strategy around the customer journey – the process we take people through to help them move from simply being aware we exist to building trust and relationship to inviting them to work with us.

Based on the consumer psychology of buyer readiness, this process helps ensure that your marketing system is continuously moving people through the journey, step by step.

Customer Journey

Attract → Engage → Nurture → Invite → Delight

The core stages of the Customer Journey include::

Stage 1:: Attract

These are the marketing activities that help you bring awareness of you, your brand, and your message to new audiences. Attract strategies that align best with Mentors include building relationships with other connectors and influencers to create a network of referral sources and opportunities to connect with their communities.

Connecting:: As a Mentor, you probably have a wide circle of friends, colleagues, and acquaintances that you've acquired over the years. Now is the time to start getting more intentional and focused on who you need to connect with. Do you need to connect with influencers who can introduce you to new audiences? Do you need to connect with potential referral sources or collaborators? Make connecting with new people a priority on your marketing calendar.

Referral Partners:: As you build your network, look for opportunities to build a referral network with other business owners who serve a similar audience. A strong referral network is built on understanding what the other has to offer and who you can serve so take time to get to know your referral partners and their business. You might consider offering a referral fee for each referral that becomes a client or simply promoting each other to your individual communities via your newsletter list. The opportunities to collaborate are endless!

Referral Events:: Co-hosting events are a fantastic way to introduce yourself to new communities. These events do not have to be over-the-top! They could be as simple as a 30 minute lunch and learn workshop or customer appreciation event hosted to your referral partners top clients. For example, a yoga teacher might host short *yoga for runners* workshop for a running community as an introduction to your work.

Stage 2:: Engage

Once you've been introduced to new potential clients, the next step is to officially engage them with your business. How? By adding them to your database.

For smart Mentors, your database is hands down the most important asset for the long term growth of your business. This database includes, of course, email addresses so you can begin to nurture these potential clients on a regular basis.

You'll also want to keep more detailed records as people become more engaged with your business so you can offer more high-touch communication with a personalized touch.

Stage 3:: Nurture

The majority of the relationship building is done in this stage of the Customer Journey. This is where you offer free useful, helpful content that helps your dream clients to start experiencing some small wins, establish trust with you, and move towards becoming paying clients.

Mentors can do well with essentially any platform – social media, emails, blogs, podcasts, or video – as long as there is an opportunity for your potential clients to connect with you on a more personal level.

How can you connect with your potential clients? It could be as simple as asking them to reply to your email newsletters, asking questions at the end of your blog posts, or hosting live Q&A calls. Whether in person or online, your marketing strategy works best when you're engaged with your community.

Content:: Your goal with content on any platform is to offer useful, relevant information that helps people to *try on* your approach to achieving results. Once you win them over with a few small wins in a supportive environment, they will get more excited about the prospect of working with you.

Community:: Whether hosting in-person events or simply hosting a Facebook group, you will stand out when you are leveraging your talent for bringing people together. Remember, engagement starts with you! Map out a calendar for your engagement plan to ensure that your community maintains connection to you.

Stage 4:: Invite

You have to actually invite people to take that next step and pay for your products, programs, and services. For Mentors, this often means having a clear invitation strategy that not only builds excitement, but allows people a high-touch opportunity to connect with you.

Invitation Conversations:: While people will buy low-touch offerings such as information products without a conversation, when it comes to working with you for high-touch programs and services, you'll want to talk with your dream clients. These conversations don't need to be pushy sales-conversations! They simply are an opportunity to confirm that your potential client is a perfect fit for what you offer and how you work.

High-Touch Launches:: As you start to scale your business, you'll need to move from selling via one-on-one conversations to one-to-many conversations. As a Mentor, you can integrate your high touch approach into online launches {such as video series or challenges} by including access to you for live Q&A from your community.

Stage 5:: Delight

Delight is where Mentors shine! This is the stage where most stop thinking about marketing – but when you design and deliver an incredible customer experience, you'll see more rave reviews, referrals, and repeat business.

Impeccable Customer Experience. If you want not only happy clients, but long term clients who rave about you to their friends, family, and colleagues, experience is essential. A fantastic experience isn't just about fun gifts – it's all about clear communication, expectations, and anticipating the needs of your clients. This is where you not just do what you were hired to do – but go the extra mile. The more your clients feel like you're fully in control and you've got their back, the happier they will be.

Referrals. Referrals are everything. EVERYTHING! Especially for Mentors who do deep, transformational work. Referrals allow you to focus on what you do best and build a solid reputation. These can come from clients or referral partners, however sitting back and waiting for referrals to come your way isn't going to cut it. You've got to ASK for the referrals. Make a plan to followup with all your clients, host client appreciation events, and offer incentives for your best referring clients.

Repeat Business. When you develop meaningful relationships with your clients, you'll find that they will be loyal to you for life. Consider how many clients you need to build a solid customer base and design your offerings to encourage your clients to continue working with you for the long term.

Mastermind

As the kid who always sold the most wrapping paper for the school fundraiser, Sue knew she liked making sales. She went on to become an award winning saleswoman for everything from linens for hotels to medical devices for hospitals.

It was no surprise when she started training Fortune 500 sales managers, but it was a surprise when the high-stress started to affect her health. She left her sales job and started a blog about managing stress. Thanks to her background in sales, Sue already understood why she needed a clear strategy for her blog to generate revenue.

After a few years of blogging in the stress management niche, Sue blended her blogging and sales experience into her newest venture Successful Blogging. It was the perfect next step for a Mastermind with a lifetime of sales experience to serve a new audience.

ARE YOU A MASTERMIND?

If you're a natural problem solver like Sue, your Business Sweet Spot centers around taking complex information and teaching us the step by step process to achieve our goals. Combined with their natural curiosity and desire to learn, Masterminds love diving into research then synthesizing it into actionable lessons.

As a Mastermind, you are wired to take in and sift through lots of information. In fact, chances are nothing makes you happier than learning new things and finding new connections.

When there is a problem to be solved, you have no doubt that you can find the solution.

And when Plan A fails, you can quickly come up with plans B-Z. You naturally see solutions to problems your clients struggle with... in fact, you might see the solutions so clearly that it's easy to discount the value you bring to the table.

Masterminds are the problem solvers of the world. You see the steps that uncomplicate the process of learning how we can achieve our goals.

WE WANT YOU TO TEACH US

People reach out to Masterminds when they are overwhelmed with choices or unsure of the right decision. They lean on your expertise to simplify decision-making and help them get momentum toward their goals by having a clear plan to follow.

The most successful Masterminds leverage their expertise by synthesizing the best of what they know for others. Their dream clients look to them to do all the research and testing, then give them the Cliff's Notes version on the topic.

MASTERMIND STRENGTHS

1:: Curiosity

The most successful Masterminds are students first. Even if they weren't straight A students in formal school, they have a natural curiosity and thirst for knowledge that continues throughout their lifetime.

When you get excited about a topic, you become nearly obsessed. When a Mastermind is interested in a topic, they devour everything they can get their hands on. They read, they attend workshops, the listen to other great teachers. People quickly know you as the go-to for questions in that topic.

2:: Strategic Thinking

We come to you when we need to be focused on the future. When we come to you with a dream, you help us turn it into an actionable goal. When we are struggling to solve a problem ourselves, we turn to you to shorten our learning curve. You have the unique ability to not only see the path to reach our goals, but also see the alternative routes when roadblocks arise.

3:: Synthesizer

When you dive into a new topic, you take in information from as many sources as possible. Where others might be overwhelmed with so much input and information, as you dive into your research, you naturally start to see trends and love sharing the highlights with others.

A word of caution – your excitement for all the information will overwhelm everyone else! Learn to edit down your insights to the most essential lessons that will help your clients to see the results they are looking for.

MASTERMIND STRUGGLES

1:: Isolation

Many Masterminds spend too much time in their creative cave creating content or courses without testing their theories with REAL people. If you want to turn your knowledge and experience into a business, it's crucial that you start by getting those ideas into action.

Working 1×1 or in small groups will help you validate your ideas, navigate obstacles, and ensure that your students get results. Look at your products, programs, and services as experiments that need multiple iterations to hone your signature process.

2:: Perfectionism

Masterminds often struggle to feel ready to share their offerings – leading to offerings never launching due to endless tweaking and non-stop research.

Your focus is on progress not perfection! It's better to launch an imperfect offering that you can upgrade later than to hold back from helping your dream clients right now.

3:: Not Enoughness

Many Masterminds hold themselves back because they worry about being expert enough. When a Mastermind doubts her expertise, her first thought is "*I need more training! I need a credential! I need another degree!*"

You don't need to be a PhD in your topic area to serve others. Remember that expertise is relative. Even on a scale of 1-10, if you are a 4, there are plenty of 1, 2, and 3s you can help. Start exactly where you are – even if it's just sharing your ideas with a few people!

MASTERMIND PROSPERITY PLAN

Many Masterminds find the most opportunity for growth through multimedia platforms that allow them to reach and teach people around the world.

The foundational element for your platform? Developing a signature system that helps your dream clients learn how they can step-by-step solve their problem.

As you design your signature system, leverage your Mastermind strengths to uncomplicate the process for your clients. It's essential to work with clients as you design your signature system as often, Masterminds struggle with the curse of expertise.

Once you have a signature system in place that delivers consistent results for your clients, you can distribute it at multiple price points and levels of accessibility by building a teaching platform. A teaching platform places your methodology out into the hands of as many people in as many different formats as possible.

There are many opportunities to leverage your signature product or program::

- Information Products {Books, DVDs, CDs}
- Online Courses & Programs
- Live Training Events
- High-End Consulting
- Certification or Train the Trainer Programs
- Licensing Programs

As a Mastermind, your business has a singular focus:: reaching and teaching as many people as possible!

MARKETING FOR MASTERMINDS

As a Mastermind, you're naturally wired to be a great teacher. Enter education based marketing that leverages your expertise across multiple formats and mediums.

In Sweet Spot Strategy, we design your entire marketing strategy around the customer journey – the process we take people through to help them move from hearing about us for the first time to joining our products, programs, and services.

Based on the consumer psychology of buyer readiness, this process helps ensure that your marketing system is continuously moving people through the journey, step by step.

Customer Journey

Attract » Engage » Nurture » Invite » Delight

The core stages of the Customer Journey include::

Stage 1:: Attract

These are the marketing activities that help you bring awareness of you, your brand, and your message to new audiences. Masterminds find they can reach and teach new audiences best when they get an opportunity to share their insights by contributing articles, interviews, and guest teaching.

Contributing Articles & Guest Posts:: One of the best ways to boost your exposure and gain credibility is contributing articles and guest blog posts to well-read newspapers, magazines, and blogs. Thanks to the rise in online content, demand for fresh new content is incredibly high. Look for outlets in your niche that regularly feature new contributors to boost your traffic, credibility, and social proof.

Interviews:: If you enjoy speaking off the cuff, interviews can be a fantastic alternative to contributing articles and guest posts. With podcasting becoming an incredibly popular platform, with new podcasts popping up in nearly every niche, it's incredibly easy to pitch yourself as an expert interview and get in front of new audiences. Another plus to podcast interviews? Once you get a few under your belt, your podcasting credibility makes it even easier to get more interview opportunities.

Guest Teaching:: As a Mastermind, teaching is one of your strengths! Leverage your knack for teaching by looking for opportunities to teach in front of new audiences. This can take the form of co-hosting in person workshops or online webinars. An even more powerful way to get in front of your dream clients? Offer your expertise as a guest expert inside a complimentary experts existing training or online course.

Stage 2::: Engage

Engage is the stage of the customer journey where your potential clients take the step towards becoming a part of your community. How? They take the step from learning about you to joining your email list.

Why an email list? This database is your greatest marketing asset that you can leverage to not only build a dedicated audience, but also use to communicate your latest products, programs, and services.

Stage 3:: Nurture

The majority of the relationship building is done in this stage of the Customer Journey. This is where you provide relevant, useful, practical information that educates your audience and helps them to start taking action to see results.

As natural teachers, Masterminds do extremely well with content marketing strategies across multiple platforms including blogging, podcasting, and videos. With a consistent content creation calendar in place, a Mastermind can quickly use content marketing as a way to test and validate their ideas and get feedback from a living, breathing audience.

As a mastermind, your goal to resonate deeply with your audience, with your community, isn't to market to them. It's to teach them. It's to give them some practical strategies, tools and techniques that they can use to start this journey.

Blogging:: It almost seems that blogging was designed for Masterminds! Some of the most popular content on the internet for nearly every niche is dominated by *How To* blog posts that walk readers step-by-step to achieve results.

Podcasts:: If your audience prefers to learn on the go, podcasting could be a fantastic platform. Podcasts can have a range of show formats – from solo shows where you discuss a single topic to inviting a co-host to talk with you to interviewing guests – there is a lot of variety available for you to showcase your expertise.

Video:: If your audience would get the most out of seeing you demonstrate something, video is another fantastic option. You could film yourself walking through a process {think cooking shows or makeup tutorials} or if your topic is more technical, you could record your screen walking people step-by-step through a process on their computer.

Stage 4:: Invite

You've done a fantastic job building your reputation and building an audience. Next you need to invite people to take that next step and join your products, programs, and services. For Masterminds, this a solid invitation strategy that helps your audience see that you are the right teacher for them.

Mini-Trainings:: Want to offer a taste of what to expect inside your product or program? A mini-training could be the perfect option. Simply pull together 3-5 key lessons that offer a peek into what they will learn with small action step that allows them to start seeing results right away. These lessons can be shared in nearly any format, including::

- Email Series
- Blog Series
- Podcast Series
- Video Series

Workshops & Webinars:: Masterminds struggle with many traditional marketing and sales strategies when then feel more like a performer than a teacher. That's why workshops and webinars work incredibly well for Masterminds – they allow you to showcase your greatest gifts!

If you are a local entrepreneur, in-person workshops are a fantastic way to establish yourself in your community. Free or paid, workshops are a great way to introduce your work and attract dream 1×1 clients.

Webinars allow you to make workshops available to anyone, anywhere. The same concept applies – teach amazing content and invite people to work with you!

Stage 5:: Delight

Once someone has started your product, program, or service, you'll want to ensure they not only see results, but share rave reviews about their experience.

Delight is all about surprising and delighting your clients by providing an amazing customer experience that has those people coming back for more. While many entrepreneurs focus on attracting as many people as possible into their businesses, it's important to keep in mind that it's 7X more expensive to attract a new client than to keep an existing one!

Design your offerings with a stellar experience so they don't collect dust on the virtual shelf. When you take the time to engage your clients, not only will you see more amazing results from your students, but those students will continue coming back to you for higher level programs and services.

People want to know that your process delivers RESULTS. That's one reason case students, testimonials, and other social proof are essential. They show your credibility and expertise. This works especially well when you can use visual storytelling or share clear before + afters {for example, a money mindset coach sharing her student's best month ever stories}. Sharing those aspirational stories of your clients will go a long way in people believing you can do the same for them.

About The Author

Racheal Cook, MBA is a green smoothie enthusiast, restorative yoga advocate, and award winning business strategist who believes entrepreneurs can grow their dream business while living their dream life, right now.

After experiencing debilitating anxiety and burnout in her former life in the traditional corporate world, Racheal walked away from a lucrative consulting career and onto a yoga mat. Months later, she married her passion for yoga and business acumen by launching The Yogipreneur, a boutique consultancy teaching the yoga of business and mindful marketing.

Since launching TheYogipreneur.com in 2008

and RachealCook.com in 2014, she's built two multiple six-figure businesses inspiring over 20,000 entrepreneurs around the world to create profitable, sustainable businesses they can be proud of, all while navigating the beautiful chaos of raising three kids, two kittens, and one cocker spaniel with her husband Jameson.

Her work has been featured on Female Entrepreneur Association, Smart Passive Income, The Rise to The Top, and Entrepreneur on Fire.

When she's not sharing her latest insights on business and lifestyle design, you can find Racheal practicing yoga with her three kidlets, reading everything she can get her hands on, and experimenting with new green smoothie recipes {spinach, avocado, and pineapple are her fav!}.

Visit Racheal's home on the web at RachealCook.com.

More From Racheal Cook

If you loved this book, you'll find more of my work here!

Fired Up & Focused
http://amzn.to/2b41J55

My first book takes the best lessons from my 21 Day Fired Up & Focused Challenge to help you plan, prioritize, and boost your productivity in your business. You'll get excited about your business again – because you'll kiss stress and busywork goodbye. You'll be doing the right things ... at the right time ... the right way.

Sunday Insights

If you'd like to be the first to know about when my next book comes out, plus get weekly insights into designing a business you love {with a lifestyle to match}, sign up here for my weekly insights: http://www.rachealcook.com/.

Take The Quiz

READY FOR MORE EASE & LESS STRESS IN YOUR BUSINESS?
IT ALL BEGINS WITH UNLOCKING YOUR BUSINESS SWEET SPOT.

You don't have to squeeze your business into someone else's model for success. Your business should be designed around *YOU!*

Answer a few short questions *based on what you do best* to discover your Business Sweet Spot and receive a custom Sweet Spot Guide with key insights and inspired action steps to grow your business with elegance and ease. You'll discover –

- How your Business Sweet Spot Theme can

help you leverage your innate strengths and help you work smarter, not harder, as you leverage your highest value in your business.

- An instant assessment of where you currently are in your business journey and learn the top priorities should focus on right now, based on your Business Sweet Spot Theme.

- Exclusive Sweet Spot Theme guide sharing recommendations and next-steps to reach your goals {finally – a roadmap to build your business, your way!}.

Take the Business Sweet Spot Quiz to get customized advice + business training! http://www.rachealcook.com/quiz/

Deep Gratitude

There have been many people who have helped me along this entrepreneurial journey, but I must give deep gratitude first to my amazing parents. Growing up with two entrepreneurs shapes your perspective about the world and your role in it. Thank you for helping me understand and discover my sweet spot so early in life!

All my love to my incredible husband, Jameson, for being my strongest supporter and biggest cheerleader, and my amazing children, Alex, Juli, and Mitchell, who inspire me daily to keep working to make the world a better place for them to grow up in.

Thank you to my team:: Lane Clark-Bonk, Amber Kinney, Kayla Rose, and Katie

Truman. I'm constantly amazed at how talented each of you are and can't believe how lucky I was to find you!

And to all my amazing students of Sweet Spot Strategy. You inspired this work by challenging me to think about your businesses in new ways. Thank you for helping me to create Your Business Sweet Spot!

Printed in Great Britain
by Amazon